MW01252446

Certified Professional Secretary®
Self-Study Guide
Office Systems
and Administration

Fourth Edition

Certified Professional Secretary® Self-Study Guides

Betty L. Schroeder, *Series Editor*

Schroeder, Clark, Dimarzio, Lewis, and Webber, *Certified Professional Secretary® Review for Finance and Business Law*, Fourth Edition

Cherry, *Self-Study Guide to CPS® Review for Finance and Business Law*, Fourth Edition

Schroeder and Kardoff, *Certified Professional Secretary® Review for Management*, Fourth Edition

Cherry, *Self-Study Guide to CPS® Review for Management*, Fourth Edition

Schroeder and Graf, *Certified Professional Secretary® Review for Office Systems and Administration*, Fourth Edition

Cherry, *Self-Study Guide to CPS® Review for Office Systems and Administration*, Fourth Edition

CERTIFIED PROFESSIONAL SECRETARY®
SELF-STUDY GUIDE

OFFICE SYSTEMS
AND ADMINISTRATION

Fourth Edition

Janet T. Cherry, Ed.D., CPS
Performance Improvement Consulting
Memphis, Tennessee

A joint publication of
INTERNATIONAL ASSOCIATION OF ADMINISTRATIVE PROFESSIONALS

and

PRENTICE HALL
Upper Saddle River, New Jersey 07458-1813

Executive Editor: *Elizabeth Sugg*
Managing Editor: *Judy Casillo*
Editorial Assistant: *Anita Rhodes*
Production Editor: *Eileen O'Sullivan*
Managing Editor: *Mary Carnis*
Manufacturing Buyer: *Cathleen Petersen*
Director of Manufacturing & Production: *Bruce Johnson*
Marketing Manager: *Tim Peyton*
Cover Design: *Joe Sengotta*
Printer/Binder: *Banta Harrisonburg*

© 2001, 1995, 1992, 1984 by Prentice-Hall, Inc.
Upper Saddle River, New Jersey 07458

All rights reserved. No part of this book may be reproduced, in any form or by any means, without permission in writing from publisher.

The following are registered marks owned by the International Association of Administrative Professionals™:

Trademarks and Registered Service Marks

IAAP™
International Association of Administrative Professionals™ (formerly Professional Secretaries International®)
10502 N.W. Ambassador Drive, Kansas City, MO 64153, 816-891-6600

A.I.S.P. (French equivalent of PSI®)
L'Association Internationale des Secretaries Professionailes

CPS®
Certified Professional Secretary®

CSI^SM
Collegiate Secretaries International^SM
Professional Secretaries Week®
Professional Secretaries Day®
Office PRD®

FSA®
Future Secretaries Association®
International Secretary of the Year®
Secretary Speakout®
Secretary on the Spot®

Printed in the United States of America

10 9 8 7 6 5 4 3 2 1

ISBN 0-13-030030-6

Prentice-Hall International (UK) Limited, *London*
Prentice-Hall of Australia Pty, Limited, *Sydney*
Prentice-Hall Canada, Inc., *Toronto*
Prentice-Hall Hispanoamericana, S.A., *Mexico*
Prentice-Hall of India Private Limited, *New Delhi*
Prentice-Hall of Japan, Inc., *Tokyo*
Pearson Education Asia, Pte. Ltd., *Singapore*
Editora Prentice-Hall do Brasil, Ltda., *Rio de Janeiro*

CONTENTS

SUGGESTIONS FOR USING THIS SELF-STUDY GUIDE

This Self-Study Guide is written as a personal learning tool and is a companion to the Prentice Hall CPS® Review Manual. There is no section in the Guide with suggested answers. The Guide does, however, consistently follow the content in the Review Manual. The objective of the Self-Study Guide is to assist you in researching and building your own information bank.

Make the Self-Study Guide your special workbook to put in writing the information you have acquired through reading the Prentice Hall CPS Review Manual, attending review classes, participating in group study sessions, and from other informational sources. When you have completed all of the exercises in the Guide, return to the text and check out your answers. Correct any items you may not have answered fully or correctly. When this is done, you will have an excellent study source. Instructors for the CPS Review Courses often use the Self-Study Guide as part of class materials.

As an independent study resource, consider the following steps:

• Scan the table of contents of both the Guide and the Manual.

• Read the first section of the companion Review Manual. When you feel comfortable with the text material, take out the Guide and complete the appropriate pages. Continue this pattern throughout the book.

• Set your own pace. You are in control of your study plan.

• If certain items are confusing to you, or you just don't remember the topic, return to the Module and read it again. By writing your answers, you will be reinforcing your awareness of specific facts in each section.

• Begin to **S-T-E-P** through a daily review. Make copies of the **S-T-E-P** (Study Tip Exam Prep) cards that are found in the back of the Self-Study Guide. Keep the copies with you at all times—in your pockets, beside your bed, in your car, and at your desk. Learn three facts about each term on the cards. Record the terms on a cassette tape, leaving time between words for you to mentally give definitions and facts about each, and play the tapes at home or in your car for a quick mental quiz.

• FastFact cards are also in the back of this Self-Study Guide. Remove the cards and cut them into pocketsize cards along the line provided. Use the cards to help you become familiar with terminology from the CPS Review Manual. Record the information from the cards onto a cassette tape, and play the tape as often as you can (in other words until you become totally tired of it!) for additional reinforcement.

Accelerated Group Review Course

The materials contained in this Self-Study Guide are also a valuable study tool for formal or informal groups. Informal groups might include noon, evening, or intense weekend study sessions.

The informal groups usually function best when the leadership role is shared. A workable plan is to allow each participant to volunteer for a particular section of the CPS® Outline and Bibliography. The section leader provides information to the group about each outline topic—try to provide three facts about each topic. Group members should also rotate as moderators for a quiz on terminology using either the FastFact cards or the **S-T-E-P** cards.

It's time to begin. Enjoy your journey toward Certification!

ADDITIONAL SUGGESTIONS FOR PREPARING FOR THE CPS® EXAMINATION

CONGRATULATIONS! The mere fact that you are reading this page is a sure sign that you have made a commitment to attain certification. You are to be applauded.

Over the years candidates for the examination have offered suggestions—and I have added a few of my own—for how to prepare yourself for success. It is a pleasure to share them with you.

• Find yourself a hide-away where interruptions are minimal. Go there on a planned schedule. Of course there will be days when this just can't happen, but try very hard not to accept your own excuses for not sticking with your study plan.

• Practice speed-reading and comprehension. These are valuable skills to have on exam day.

• Check the publication dates on resources you pick up to read. This is particularly true with articles/books on technology. Read only about the latest techniques and processes.

• Find a mentor—an office professional who has already earned certification. A person who has "been there, done that" will know what you are going through and can give you a boost when the goal you have set for yourself seems overwhelming.

• Be prepared to deal with negative reactions you might encounter. Stay in control of your decisions, your time, and your career goals. The CPS® rating is an excellent investment in you.

• Attend trade shows, read industry magazines, search the web, and scan office product catalogues for terms, trends, and information.

• Don't procrastinate! Outline a study plan and STICK TO IT! Stay current with your review topics. The week of the examination will come before you know it—YOU WILL BE READY IF YOU WORK AT PREPARING FOR THE EXAM ONE DAY AT A TIME.

• Most importantly, get your examination application completed and mailed by the deadline. Applications are available without charge from:

IAAP Certification Department
1052 NW Ambassador Drive
PO Box 20404
Kansas City, MO 64195-0404
Tel: 816-891-6600   FAX: 816-891-9118
E-mail: cps@iaap-hq.org
Web Site: www.iaap-hq.org

TO THE CPS® CANDIDATE

Congratulations on your decision to become a Certified Professional Secretary!

The materials in this Self-Study Guide were prepared to follow the outline and bibliography published by the Institute for Certification, a department of the International Association of Administrative Professionals (IAAP). This is one of the three Self-Study Guides in the series—there is one for each of the three CPS Review Manuals published by Prentice Hall in conjunction with IAAP™.

The information in each of the Self-Study Guides is intended to help you to focus your study of the material in the review manuals. Use the information to become more familiar with the terminology, associations, similarities, and differences in the material in the three-part series.

The primary objective of any review course or of any review manual is to serve as a "thought processor" to bring to the surface certain knowledge, skills, and abilities that may have become subconsciously stored away. It is expected that a candidate for the CPS Examination would possess the basic fundamentals and skills related to topics covered in each module. If this knowledge base is not present, you may consider enrolling in an introductory course at a post-secondary institution to develop that base.

The Self-Study Guides should be used in conjunction with the appropriate CPS Review Manuals.

ACKNOWLEDGMENTS

It is a pleasure to be associated with the continuous learning efforts of office professionals. From personal experience as an executive assistant for some 12 years, I respect the contributions office professionals make to the success of our global economy. My personal passion for learning and the support of previous managers, teachers, mentors, colleagues, and family have nurtured the seeds for this series. I am particularly grateful to the following individuals.

The instructors who use and critique the Self-Study Guide Series;

The Institute for Certification, the International Board of the International Association of Administrative Professionals, and the IAAP staff for their interest in and support of these materials;

Elizabeth Sugg and Judy Casillo, Prentice Hall, for their patience and guidance throughout this project;

F. Grant Whittle, whose desktop publishing skills are evidenced throughout this manual;

Secretaries around the world with their thirst for professionalism and knowledge who encourage and inspire me to improve these materials with each edition; and

The person who introduced me to membership in professional associations, served as my role model for an office professional, encouraged me to earn my certification and educational degrees, and to whom this series is dedicated, my mother.

INTRODUCTION

OFFICE SYSTEMS AND ADMINISTRATION

Office Administration/Communication and Office Systems are the most commonly familiar sections of the certification examination. Topics focus on the routine, directive, and creative tasks outlined in office and secretarial procedures manuals and textbooks, and listed in position descriptions for office professionals.

Directed tasks require the command of traditional office procedures. Creative tasks call for the combination of sound theory and the knowledge of possibilities and probabilities of electronic technology. While this does provide "common ground," so to speak, don't be misled into believing that this part deserves less of your attention. Remember, routine tasks become individual and specific tasks within a particular organizational environment. Use your own experiences as "a" resource but not "the" resource for making your answer decisions. Although the answer provided in the CPS Review Manual may not parallel the practice followed in your office, it is the basic philosophy generally practiced. This examination and the preparation materials are addressing people, office situations, cultural, and industry differences world wide.

The Communication chapters follow fundamentals of accepted letter and report writing and editing techniques. Again, the format used in your office will be the most familiar; however, for examination preparation you will also want to recall and recognize communication practices that are not a part of your administrative processes and procedures.

Overall, you are expanding your internal "resource shelf," and long after the examination is over you will benefit from increasing your knowledge, skills, and abilities as a professional.

Together, the mastery of office systems and office administration/communication make the difference between the office worker and the office professional.

Janet T. Cherry, Ed.D., CPS

SECTION I: OFFICE TECHNOLOGY
CHAPTER 1: INFORMATION PROCESSING

Information processing involves both data processing and word processing, data referencing data input, information referencing output.

The Processing Cycle

The major function of business data processing is to take unorganized facts (data) and process them to produce meaningful business information. The basic processing cycle consists of input, process, and output. The six steps of the cycle involve:

1.

2.

3.

4.

5.

6.

Give examples of business transactions processed as a group:

Real-time processing is . . .

A source document is . . .

The need for a source document is eliminated when . . .

1

Hardware configurations can include:

1.

2.

3.

4.

The length of time required for processing will depend on:

1.

2.

3.

4.

Turnaround time is . . .

Data are stored as records. Define the following terms associated with records.

File

Record

Data fields

Key fields

2

The printed report is called_____copy.

Viewing output on the CRT screen is_____copy.

Processing Technology

Computer technology has gone through five generations of change. Included in the technology are:

1.

2.

3.

4.

Give a brief summary of the characteristics of the five generations of computers.

First generation

Second generation

Third generation

3

Fourth generation

Fifth generation

The equipment used in processing data is called _____.

The ( ) digital ( ) analog computer is used to organize numbers. The ( ) digital ( ) analog computer is used as a measuring device.

Make statements about the elements of the electronic computer system which are listed below.

Input devices

Secondary-storage devices

Output devices

Processor unit

The central processing unit (CPU) is the heart of a computer system. It consists of:

1.

2.

4

The duty of the CPU is to . . .

Fetching refers to . . .

The arithmetic unit performs _____computations and
_____ comparisons.

Arithmetic operations can be performed only on ( ) numeric ( ) numeric/alphabetic/special characters.
Logical operations can be performed only on ( ) numeric or ( ) numeric/alphabetic/special characters.

Name the three categories of computer systems:

1.

2.

3.

The fourth computer category, used by the military and large organizations, is called the . . .

The microprocessor is the technology of the_____.

The basic additional components of the microcomputer system include:

1.

2.

3.

Input devices allow human beings to communicate with the computer. Input media are the physical
material on which data are recorded. Make statements about the examples of input media listed below.

Punched card

Punched paper tape

Magnetic disk packs

Hard disks

Diskettes

Optical disks

Magnetic-ink character recognition

Optical recognition

Remote input

Equipment used to prepare the input media and/or transmit the data to the computer is known as hardware.

Direct entry takes place whenever a person enters data directly into the computer without intervention from an input medium. Common direct-entry devices are:

1.

2.

3.

4.

5.

6.

7.

8.

A user interface is a combination of hardware and software that makes data input easier. A user interface allows a user to respond to messages presented by the computer, control the computer, and request information from the computer. Examples of interfaces include:

1.

2.

3.

4.

Examples of output media are:

The output document produced on paper is called_____.

The appropriateness of a printer or printing device for information processing output will depend on:

1.

2.

3.

4.

Classify each of the printers listed below as an impact printer or a nonimpact printer:

Printer	Impact	Nonimpact
Line		
Chain		
Ink jet		
Dot matrix		
Serial		
Laser		
Drum		
Fiber optics		
Intelligent		

Background printing is . . .

A special-purpose printer, known as a _____, outlines drawings.

COM means . . .

A **modem** is a device for . . .

Primary storage is the ( ) internal ( ) external storage of the processor unit. It is also referred to as main memory.

Metal oxide semiconductor memory (MOS), the most prevalent internal memory in use today is ( ) volatile or ( ) nonvolatile.

Internal memory that is available to the user is ( ) random access memory (RAM) or ( ) read-only (ROM) memory.

RAM ( ) is ( ) is not lost when the electrical power to the unit is turned off.

( ) Volatile or ( ) nonvolatile storage is erased/lost when the electrical power to the unit is turned off.

Bubble memory is an example of ( ) volatile or ( ) nonvolatile memory.

If you add cache memory to a computer system, you are probably wanting to significantly increase the system's _____.

A **channel** is . . .

A **port** is . . .

Explain the difference between a file that is sequentially accessed and a file that is accessed directly.

Sequentially

Directly

Access time refers to . . .

Zip and _____ disk cartridges offer _____ and fast access features of _____ disks and the portability of a single disk.

The most common media used for secondary storage are _____ tape and magnetic disk.

Software is . . .

The specific system software program that manages the computer resources is referred to as the _____ _____.

A **database** is described as . . .

The purpose of language translators (or compilers) is . . .

The five levels of programming languages are:

1.

2.

3.

4.

5.

Procedural-oriented languages place emphasis on the logic and computational steps required to solve a problem. Name and make statements about the widely used procedural languages listed below:

1.

2.

3.

4.

Object-oriented programming (OOP) languages include:

1.

2.

3.

OOPs gained popularity with the proliferation of graphic user interfaces (GUIs) in the
_____ environment and the _____ _____ _____.

Processing Operations, Concepts, and Applications

Indicate below the flow of basic operations for data processing to process business data.

1.

2.

3.

4.

5.

6.

7.

8.

9.

10.

There are two ways of processing input data: real-time processing and batch processing. Make statements about each.

Real-time

Batch

Multiprocessing means . . .

11

Teleprocessing is . . .

Networking provides . . .

Common end-user software applications include:

1.

2.

3.

4.

5.

6.

A **network is** . . .

Network processing software performs the following basic functions:

1.

2.

3.

4.

A local area network is . . .

Name and make statements about the network configurations illustrated below.

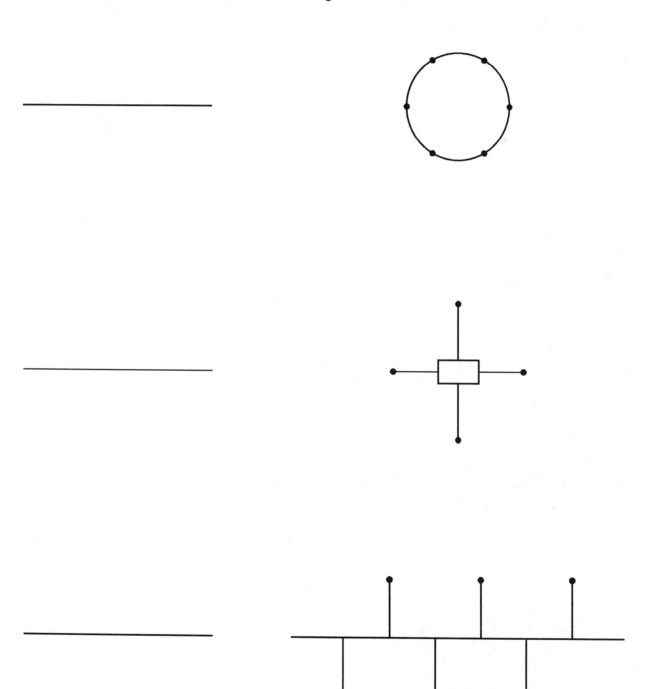

Innovations in Information Processing

Make statements about the trends in information processing that affect business functions.

1.

2.

3.

4.

CHAPTER 1: INFORMATION PROCESSING

Terms and Definitions

Use this page to record terms and definitions you want to concentrate on, or to record additional information you have located from other resources.

CHAPTER 1: INFORMATION PROCESSING

Additional Comments

Use this page to record information found in readings, notes from lectures, or notes to yourself about information to be researched.

CHAPTER 1: INFORMATION PROCESSING

Additional Comments

CHAPTER 2: WORD/INFORMATION PROCESSING

The use of the computer and the application of word processing software has provided great changes in the office. This change has left its mark on the documents produced as well as the persons preparing the documents.

Word processing, as is true of all systems, has three primary components. These components are:

1.

2.

3.

Of these three, _____ are considered the most important.

_____ _____, as a part of the total information processing effort within an organization, is the most commonly used software application.

Word Processing

Word processing is . . .

Word-processing personnel need to have a middle to high level of competence in these skills:

1.

2.

3.

4.

5.

Word/Information Processing Personnel

The person for whom a document is prepared is known as the _____ _____.

18

Compare the duties of a word processing support person to the administrative support person.

Word processing support specialist

Administrative or **executive assistant**

Career opportunities within the word processing areas mentioned below might include:

Supervisory personnel

Management personnel

Trainers

Consulting

Sales/marketing/technical support

Systems analysis

Technical writing

Temporary or part-time employment

Technology

Input systems may be either _____ or _____.

The majority of documents still originate in _____ form.

Media that store the dictator's voice for later transcription use ( ) analog ( ) digital technology. When oral information is converted into digital pulses and then stored on disks rather than cassette tapes, ( ) digital ( ) analog technology is being used to store the information.

Portable dictation units store information on . . .

Describe a centralized dictation system.

OCR means . . .

Random access is a method of storage through which information is stored in . . .

There are three categories of transcription systems on the market. Give the advantages and disadvantages of each category.

Discrete media systems

Advantages

Disadvantages

Digital electronic systems

Advantages

Disadvantages

Computer-aided systems

Advantages

Disadvantages

The standard components of any computer system with compatible word processing software include:

1.

2.

3.

4.

5.

The user may interface with the computer system through use of:

1.

2.

3.

The purpose of function keys on a computer keyboard is . . .

Explain the basic mouse operations named below:

Clicking

Double-clicking

Dragging

Power, tool, and memory bars can be activated as the top of a visual screen. Define these terms.

Power bar

Tool bar

Menu bar

Text that is electronically stored on magnetic media is called _____ _____.

Common forms of magnetic storage media today include:

1.

2.

3.

4.

5.

Magnetic disks (floppy disks) are available in two standard sizes. These sizes are _____ and _____.

Density is used to describe . . .

Explain the difference between a dedicated system and a microcomputer system.

Dedicated system

Microcomputer system

An **operating system** refers to . . .

GUI stands for . . .

Temporary storage means . . .

DOS means . . .

Timed backup means . . .

Examples of default values would be:

Some of the preferred software applications in business for microcomputer systems are:

1.

2.

3.

4.

5.

The size of type is measured in _____.

Leading is a format function meaning . . .

Kerning is a format function meaning . . .

A typeface is a family of type with the same basic design for each letter.
Typefaces are _____ or _____.

Images in the form of _____, _____, or _____ enhance the presentation of text.

A **database** is a collection of . . .

A spreadsheet application is an electronic version of a paper _____. A spreadsheet application can help solve almost any problem that involves numbers and formulas.

The difference in a stand-alone system and a networked system is:

Downloading means . . .

A **shared resource system** means . . .

Word/Information Processing Procedures

User procedures are necessary to assure that . . .

Document formatting considerations may include:

1.

2.

3.

4.

Individual production can be measured in terms of:

1.

2.

3.

4.

Information Processing Integration with Other Systems

Integration means . . .

The primary technologies that have the most chance of being integrated are:

1.

2.

3.

4.

5.

6.

One of the basic concepts of office automation is to key in information only _____ time.

Of primary concern with word processing is the ability to . . .

CAR means . . .

Word/Information Processing for the Future

Predictions for word/information processing for the next few years include:

1.

2.

3.

4.

5.

6.

7.

8.

9.

10.

CHAPTER 2: WORD/INFORMATION PROCESSING

Terms and Definitions

Use this page to record terms and definitions you want to concentrate on, or to record additional information you have located from other resources.

CHAPTER 2: WORD/INFORMATION PROCESSING

Additional Comments

Use this page to record information found in readings, notes from lectures, or notes to yourself about information to be researched.

CHAPTER 2: WORD/INFORMATION PROCESSING

Additional Comments

CHAPTER 3: COMMUNICATION TECHNOLOGY

Communication is vital to business, and computer-assisted communication has a major role in the office and in the marketplace. The telephone plays an integral part in this process.

The telephone, though at times irritating, is a vital part of the office and of our lives. Telephone technology has increased and improved the services offered. By integrating computer and telephone technologies, office personnel have found numerous ways to assist the decision-making and problem-solving processes.

Telephone Communications

Give examples of basic and special telephone services.

Basic services

Special services

Special telephone features include:

1.

2.

3.

4.

5.

6.

7.

Describe the standard office telephone equipment listed below:

Key/button telephone

Pager

Touch-tone telephone

Speakerphone

WATS stands for . . .

DID and **DOD** ( ) do ( ) do not require incoming calls to be answered by an attendant.

State the difference between the following WATS services:

Full business-day package

Measure-time package

The ( ) customer or ( ) company pays the charges on an IWATS service.

PBX and **PABX** ( ) do ( ) do not require incoming calls to be an attendant.

Interoffice Systems

It is a fact that a large portion of business communication is interoffice--some authors say between 50 and 80 percent. This interoffice communication is distributed internally in a variety of ways. Define and make statements about the following automated distribution systems:

Conveyor systems

Pneumatic tubes

Programmed mail cart

Electronic mail (e-mail) network

Make statements about the courier services listed below:

Air express

Bus express

Express delivery

Express mail

What does **ZIP** stand for?

What does the zip code **38117** mean?

Telecommunications

Communication can be transmitted in the form of text, voice, data, and image. List common transmission channels:

1.

2.

3.

4.

5.

The major types of teletransmission used within telecommunications are:

1.

2.

3.

WWW stands for . . .

_____ _____ translates an HTML document into a web page.

URL stands for . . .

and is . . .

The seven domains of the Internet are

1.

2.

3.

4.

5.

6.

7.

Teleconferencing and Telecommuting

The fact that we are a global society necessitates our considering alternatives to personal travel to bring people together to exchange information. One way to meet the increased demands on time and to reduce travel expenses is to hold meetings (business, sales, training) via electronic technology. Describe each of the following forms of electronic technology.

Teleconferencing

Audio conferencing

Video conferencing

Computer conferencing

Telecommuting

The purpose of the electronic blackboard is . . .

Preparations for setting up a successful electronic meeting/conference will include:

1.

2.

3.

4.

5.

6.

Electronic Mail

Mail sent electronically within a local area network or thousands of miles away is referred to as electronic mail (e-mail). Some of the features of the e-mail system are:

1.

2.

3.

4.

5.

FAX permits a document image to be transmitted in:

1.

2.

3.

Networks

A **network** is . . .

Internet activity includes the following resources:

1.

2.

3.

4.

5.

Who owns the Internet?

35

What does **e-commerce** mean?

The purpose of e-commerce is . . .

Information can also be distributed internally through a computer system in soft copy format. The difference between a **wide area network** (WAN) and a **local area network** (LAN) is . . .

Infonet, Telenet, and Tymnet are three widely used examples of _____ **value-added networks** (VATs).

Innovations and Trends in Business Communications Systems

Name and make a statement about some of the innovations and trends that will affect office communications systems in the next few years.

1.

2.

3.

4.

5.

6.

7.

8.

CHAPTER 3: COMMUNICATION TECHNOLOGY

Terms and Definitions

Use this page to record terms and definitions you want to concentrate on, or to record additional information you have located from other resources.

CHAPTER 3: COMMUNICATION TECHNOLOGY

Additional Comments

Use this page to record information found in readings, notes from lectures, or notes to yourself about information to be researched.

CHAPTER 3: COMMUNICATION TECHNOLOGY

Additional Comments

CHAPTER 4: RECORDS MANAGEMENT TECHNOLOGY

Records management is a rapidly growing area which is becoming more important due to integrated technology. By definition, records management is the application of systematic and scientific control to the recorded information that is required in the operation of an organization.

Automated Record Systems

In addition to **paper** (or traditional) document storage, an automated record system permits the user to store records in **image, digital**, or **voice** form for accurate and efficient retrieval at a later time.

An automated record system is different from a paper (traditional) system. Considerations for establishing an automated system are:

1.

2.

3.

4.

5.

6.

Explain the difference in the two types of retrieval used with an automated record system.

Document retrieval

Record data/field retrieval

Non-computer-assisted storage and retrieval systems refer to . . .

A **record** contains all data pertaining to one particular unit. A **file** refers to a unified set of data in storage. Each file contains a number of related **records**.

Automated record systems are . . .

Computer assisted storage/retrieval systems offer useful and time-saving techniques. Make a statement about the procedures listed below:

Automated indexing

Records usage

File management

Bar code indexes

Electronic filing

Electronic mail

Forms of Storage and Their Utilization

The advantages of paper storage/retrieval systems include:

1.

2.

3.

4.

The traditional paper storage system has known problems. Such paper storage problems may include:

1.

2.

3.

4.

Basic concepts affecting the changing emphasis on data management include:

1.

2.

3.

4.

Paper storage is measured in terms of . . .

The storage of documents or other data that include text, graphics, tables, and pictures is called

_____ _____.

The two technologies that comprise image storage are:

1.

2.

The _____ _____ is fast becoming the most popular image-based form of storage.

What are the primary advantages of microform systems?

1.

2.

3.

4.

5.

6.

Any record that contains reduced images on film is known as a microform. Records may be converted to microforms for space saving of up to 95 to 98 percent storage. Describe the following types of microforms.

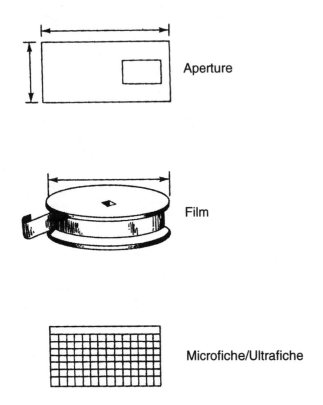

Aperture

Film

Microfiche/Ultrafiche

One example of microform packaging is shown below. Describe the **microform jacket**.

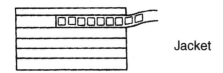

Jacket

Describe the processes shown below which are associated with microfilm.

COM

CIM

What are the advantages/disadvantages of optical-disk storage?

Advantages	Disadvantages
1.	1.
2.	2.
3.	3.
4.	4.
5.	5.
6.	6.
7.	

The most significant disadvantage of optical-disk technology is the _____ _____.

What are the legal considerations that must be met before microforms may be admitted as evidence in courts of law?

1.

2.

3.

4.

Digital storage is the form of storage within a digital computer. This type of storage processes all information in binary code.

Name and make statements about the two most common types of digital storage:

1.

2.

List the advantages/disadvantages of digital storage.

Advantages	Disadvantages
1.	1.
2.	2.
3.	3.
4.	4.

Voice storage is now being used with _____ systems and _____ devices to provide records created through the use of technology.

Equipment

Records should be stored in cabinets appropriate to the media (paper, microform, digital, or voice). The selection of equipment should be based on record content, use, value, and retention. Examples of records storage equipment are shown below. Describe the features of each type of storage cabinet pictured.

Vertical file cabinet

Lateral file cabinet

Stationary open-shelf unit

Vertical automated conveyor system

Horizontal conveyor system

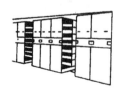

High density mobile-aisle storage unit

The most common types of equipment for storing cards include:

1.

2.

3.

4.

Special storage containers are also available for noncorrespondence items. These include:

1.   6.

2.   7.

3.   8.

4.   9.

5.   10.

Most optical disks are stored in devices called _____.

Name and define the three most commonly used microform cameras.

1.

2.

3.

Intelligent retrieval refers to . . .

The major types of equipment used in storing information in digital form are:

1.

2.

3.

4.

Optical disks may be used to store:

1.

2.

3.

4.

Computer-Based Records Management Systems

Computer-based records management systems consist of _____ and _____

_____ systems.

A **database** is . . .

The purpose of a records tracking system is . . .

CBRM means . . .

Three types of CBRM systems are:

1.

2.

3.

Basic considerations in system selection are:

1.

2.

3.

4.

5.

6.

7.

8.

9.

Integration With Other Systems

Micrographics technology and optical-disk technology provide an excellent opportunity for integration of office information systems. Computer-assisted retrieval systems (CARS) are a part of this process. Name the four primary types of CARS in operation at the present time.

1.

2.

3.

4.

Future Trends in Records Management Technology

The seven trends outlined in your Review Module are:

1.

2.

3.

4.

5.

6.

7.

Records management technology is an integral part of _____ _____ _____
(MIS) and _____ _____ _____ (OIS).

CHAPTER 4: RECORDS MANAGEMENT TECHNOLOGY

Terms and Definitions

Use this page to record terms and definitions you want to concentrate on, or to record additional information you have located from other resources.

CHAPTER 4: RECORDS MANAGEMENT TECHNOLOGY

Additional Comments

Use this page to record information found in readings, notes from lectures, or notes to yourself about information to be researched.

CHAPTER 4: RECORDS MANAGEMENT TECHNOLOGY

Additional Comments

CHAPTER 5: REPROGRAPHICS TECHNOLOGY

Reprographics technology plays an important part in the automated office. Technology has integrated various copying, duplicating, phototypesetting/composition, and imaging processes for efficiency and effectiveness in creating, storing, communicating, and distributing quality documentation.

Reprographics technology has undergone major changes in recent years. Equipment is not only cosmetically different, but the processes have changed from manual to automated; from "messy" to neat; from singular to multiple applications and features. Some of the reprographics systems that have been used in offices during the past are becoming obsolete.

Copying and Duplicating Systems

Explain the difference between the copying and duplicating processes.

Copying

Duplicating

The term **reprographics** is defined as . . .

Copiers fall into categories based on:

1.

2.

3.

Make statements about the three most common imaging processes applied in copying technology that are listed below:

Xerographic

Fiber optics

Laser

With the xerographic process, a copy is produced by projecting and image of the _____ document onto a positively charged drum.

Thermal copiers can produce:

1.

2.

3.

4.

The **diazo process** is commonly used for making copies of _____ and _____ drawings. Only documents with printing on one side can be used with this process.

The quality of laser print is comparable to . . .

Specialized copiers handle such needs as:

1.

2.

3.

The **fiber optics** copier, because of its fewer parts, tends to be:

1.

2.

The intelligent copier/printer allows the integration of reprographics operations with other automated systems. Unique and helpful features include:

1.

2.

3.

The **duplicating** process requires the preparation of a

Basic duplicating processes include:

1.

2.

3.

Although this is the most economical method for duplicating, it is becoming obsolete because . . .

Stencil duplicating is also known as _____.

Offset duplicating masters may be _____, _____, or _____

Phototypesetting and Composition Equipment

Phototypesetting is sometimes called "_____ _____" and uses photographic principles to produce typeset copy.

Two types of composition equipment available to use in composing articles, columns, or even pages for a publication include:

1.

2.

The **photo composition** process is often referred to as _____ _____ composition.

Define the following terms used by printers to indicate type size, line length, and type style.

Points

Picas

Type font

Typefaces

Desktop Publishing Systems

Hardware requirements for desktop publishing include . . .

Desktop publishing includes the ability to produce camera-ready copy for printing at one's desk. Popular features offer:

WYSIWYG means . . .

One popular desktop publishing **software** mentioned in your Review Modules is _____.

Illustrations and artwork can be scanned or redrawn using such software programs as _____ _____ or _____ _____.

Imaging Processes

Computer technology provides the opportunity to have copies, masters, or stencils prepared electronically through various imaging processes such as:

1.

2.

FAX imaging technology is used in two ways in office automation:

1.

2.

Electronic scanning processes are used for two purposes:

1.

2.

Imaging is a _____ process.

Finishing Processes

Examples of finishing processes include:

1.

2.

3.

4.

The Legal Aspects of Reprographics

Documents which are illegal to reproduce:

1.

2.

3.

4.

Copyrighted materials are defined as . . .

Textual material prepared for an employer is considered copyrighted by that employer unless . . .

The fair-use clause specified in the Copyright Law of 1976 allows limited reproduction for the following reasons:

1.

2.

3.

4.

5.

6.

Credit must always be given to the original author.

The procedure to follow in wanting to reproduce copyrighted materials is . . .

CHAPTER 5: REPROGRAPHICS TECHNOLOGY

Terms and Definitions

Use this page to record terms and definitions you want to concentrate on, or to record additional information you have located from other resources.

CHAPTER 5: REPROGRAPHICS TECHNOLOGY

Additional Comments

Use this page to record information found in readings, notes from lectures, or notes to yourself about information to be researched.

CHAPTER 5: REPROGRAPHICS TECHNOLOGY

Additional Comments

CHAPTER 6: SOFTWARE AND HARDWARE INTEGRATION

Office automation is . . .

The vital components of an office automation system are:

1.

2.

3.

Which of the above components is considered to be most important?

Organizations often use a phased approach to introduce automation. Successful implementations consider user acceptance, expertise, and creativity.

Concepts and Applications

The technologies that compose an automated system include:

1.

2.

3.

4.

Within these systems are numerous applications that will reduce repetition, increase accuracy, facilitate project management, and provide the opportunity for creative decision-making when they are applied to daily operational tasks.

A planning grid for the phased approach will assist office professionals in understanding the total efforts required and in implementing each phase successfully. Give the objectives for each phase.

OBJECTIVES

Phase 1

Introduction

Phase 2

Use of
multifunctional
devices

Phase 3

Use of
integrated
computer-based
systems

Phase 4

Introduction of
integrated
information systems

Phase 5

"Office of the Future"

The greatest potential for utilization of office automation within an organization is . . .

The manager's primary use of a workstation is to . . .

Office applications used to improve the secretary's and/or the manager's productivity include:

1.

2.

3.

4.

5.

6.

7.

Name the four strategy levels where office automation can take place.

1.

2.

3.

4.

What is the greatest advantage to the global strategy as stated in the Review Module?

Interfacing Equipment

Integration in office automation is defined as . . .

An interface is . . .

The purpose of an interface is to . . .

Integrated Software

Integrated software consists of programs that provide . . .

The benefits of integrated software include:

1.

2.

3.

4.

5.

Implications for the Future

1.

2.

3.

4.

5.

6.

7.

The implications of integration of technologies is still emerging. However, there are certain evident trends worth noting. These include:

CHAPTER 6: SOFTWARE AND HARDWARE INTEGRATION

Terms and Definitions

Use this page to record terms and definitions you want to concentrate on, or to record additional information you have located from other resources.

CHAPTER 6: SOFTWARE AND HARDWARE INTEGRATION

Additional Comments

Use this page to record information found in readings, notes from lectures, or notes to yourself about information to be researched.

CHAPTER 6: SOFTWARE AND HARDWARE INTEGRATION

Additional Comments

CHAPTER 7: ERGONOMICS

Ergonomics is the scientific study of the relationship of office employees to their physical environment, including the work space and the technology being used. The study of ergonomics is important since the environment contributes to the productivity and satisfaction of employees. Euthenics, the science of improving employee conditions through enhancing the work environment, has encouraged the study of ergonomics.

Explain each of the following bases for ergonomics:

Psychological

Physiological

Sociological

Communication theory

Rationale for Ergonomics

Environmental factors that contribute to the basis for an ergonomic environment include:

1.

2.

3.

4.

5.

An ergonomic environment is an essential element in promoting one of the basic goals of office automation. This element is . . .

Understanding Health Hazards

Employee wellness is a major concern. The environment, as well as co-workers, contribute to wellness. Identify potential problems, concerns, or complaints associated with:

Repetitive-strain, injury, or illness

Visual dysfunction

Musculoskeletal problems

Emotional disturbances

Mood disturbances

Psychosomatic disorders

Psychosocial disturbances

Research into environmental design and workplace design influencing ergonomic office systems includes the areas of:

1.

2.

3.

Ergonomic Factors

Ergonomic standards are being used in the design of office products throughout the world. These standards serve as guides for . . .

In designing the workplace, planning is critical. Not only is it necessary to plan for the appropriate flow of work and the space assigned to individuals, it is also of prime importance to incorporate into the design the comfort of the workers and the accessibility of equipment, supplies, team persons, and information to workers.

Four key ergonomic factors to be considered when planning a well-designed office conducive to peak productivity include:

1.

2.

3.

4.

Ergonomic workstations enable a secretary to be both productive and efficient. The types of activities to be performed at the workstation are an important consideration. These include the following types of tasks:

1.

2.

3.

Environmental Factors

External environmental factors (physical and psychological) such as those listed below affect the worker physically and psychologically. Make supporting statements about each of the following factors:

Lighting

Color conditioning

Sound

Proper lighting provides a safe working environment. Adequate light in the workplace results in increased productivity, better quality of work, less mental fatigue, and improved morale for the worker. Define and give examples of the types of office lighting named below:

Natural

Artificial

Task

Ambient

Fluorescent

Incandescent

A **footcandle** is . . .

The measure of **brightness** is . . .

Just as color is very important to our personal appearance and our image, so, too, does it have a major impact on our environment and on our work performance. Color psychology provides entertaining and informative reading. Studies indicate that certain colors cause specific emotional reactions in people, which are directly related to their physical environment.

The terms "warm" and "cool" are used in connection with color. Warm hues (name of a color) are associated with fire, heat, and sun. Examples of warm colors are:

What observed effect does the color **yellow** have on workers?

The color **red**?

Sound, the sensation perceived by the sense of hearing, is as common in the office as it is in other parts of our lives. Certain sounds are unique to the office environment, such as office machines and telephones and the general types of human sounds such as talking, walking, and other body movement. There may also be the sound of music in the office. Some sounds are calming and others are distracting.

Noise is unwanted sound. Sound may become noise when it is loud enough to be a nuisance.

For effective sound control, consideration should be given to materials that will **absorb, reflect**, and **isolate** sound. Explain these terms.

Absorption

Reflection

Isolation

To control noise, sound must be measured. Sound is measured in levels and expressed in decibels (dB).

The threshold of normal hearing is . . .

The average decibel level for an office is . . .

Office noises range in intensity from 20 to 90 decibels.

"White sound/noise" or "masking" refers to . . .

Make a statement about the additional environmental factors listed below which are of concern in today's offices.

Condition of the air

Surface textures, shapes, and arrangements

Control of static electricity

Power sources

Security control

Energy conservation

Worker response to the environment

Systems Analysis

Traditionally, office systems analysis seemed to focus only on the departmental functions (sales, accounting, purchasing). However, office systems analysis is now being applied to a variety of activities within the administrative arena, such as human resource planning, office layout and design, and planning for technology.

When an office system is being analyzed the three major focus areas are:

1.

2.

3.

and how these areas are involved in the particular system.

Define the term **feasibility study** and explain how it helps or relates to an office system.

Specific aspects of such a study might include:

1.

2.

3.

4.

5.

6.

7.

The person conducting a systems analysis uses a variety of "tools." In all instances, they are investigating four areas. These areas are:

1.

2.

3.

4.

Office Layout and Design

The traditional office arrangement is sometimes referred to as a _____ _____ design. The modern approach most often refers to the _____ _____ arrangement.

The open office arrangement labeled "hotelling" means . . .

In designing the workplace, planning is critical. Not only is it necessary for the appropriate flow of work and the space assigned to individuals, it is also of prime importance to incorporate into the design the comfort of the workers and the accessibility of equipment, supplies, team persons, and information to workers.

Five key ergonomic factors to be considered when planning a well-designed office conducive to peak productivity include:

1.

2.

3.

4.

5.

Ergonomic workstations enable a secretary to be both productive and efficient. The types of activities to be performed at the workstation are an important consideration. These activities include:

1.

2.

3.

The open-office arrangement is characterized by these features:

1.

2.

3.

4.

Two popular approaches for open-office arrangements are _____ _____ and the _____ _____.

An office designer has the ultimate goal of providing a space where . . .

Workflow considerations are related to information flow throughout the office. Regardless of the method of communication selected (including electronic systems), it is crucial that the workflow move in a forward direction and a straight line whenever possible.

The term meaning information flow which is a result of the type of communication system in place is _____.

Factors affecting space design include:

1.

2.

3.

4.

5.

6.

7.

Basic steps to consider when considering office space requirements are:

1.

2.

3.

4.

Design of Work Areas

Workstations are designed so that the organizational objectives can be met. The workstation must support:

1.

2.

3.

Deciding where to place specific office equipment depends on . . .

Computers should be placed directly in front of the operator to allow for working either to the _____ or _____, whichever is a more convenient arrangement.

General secretarial references that should be accessible on, in, or near the secretary's desk may include the following:

1.

2.

3.

4.

5.

6.

7.

8.

Name ways in which the workstation design and the types of office equipment selected may alleviate the discomfort of the office employee.

1.

2.

3.

4.

5.

Make statements about the following aspects of workstation design that may affect employee acceptance.

Need for territoriality

Personalizing the workstation

Social needs

Office Furniture and Equipment Procurement

The selection process for office furniture is affected by these factors:

1.

2.

3.

4.

5.

6.

7.

8.

Basic considerations for choosing office equipment include:

1.

2.

3.

4.

5.

6.

7.

8.

9.

10.

11.

Name four of the most important considerations in handling office supplies and explain why.

1.

2.

3.

4.

What does the term **outsourcing** mean?

Future Trends in Ergonomics

Make statements about each of the future trends as presented in the Review Module.

Business and Office Design

Emphasis on Quality of Work Life

Privacy Issues

Government Involvement in Development of Standards

Instead of the user adapting to the work environment, the work environment must be designed and adapted to the user.

CHAPTER 7: ERGONOMICS

Terms and Definitions

Use this page to record terms and definitions you want to concentrate on, or to record additional information you have located from other resources.

CHAPTER 7: ERGONOMICS

Additional Comments

Use this page to record information found in readings, notes from lectures, or notes to yourself about information to be researched.

CHAPTER 7: ERGONOMICS

Additional Comments

SECTION II: OFFICE ADMINISTRATION
CHAPTER 8: BUSINESS TRAVEL

For many office professionals, making arrangements for business travel is a major part of their position responsibilities. Office professionals need to be able to recognize terms associated with travel as well as the organizational policies that dictate how travel should be arranged.

Organizational Policies and Procedures for Travel

Business travelers need to follow specific procedures established by the organization in arranging authorized travel. Such procedures may include:

1.

2.

Appropriate approval for business travel and/or use of company-owned transportation is important so that business insurance policies will cover the individual in case of accident or emergency.

Approval for business travel may include such typical procedures as . . .

1.

2.

3.

4.

To schedule the use of company-owned vehicles, the traveler may be asked to complete a request form calling for the following information:

1.

2.

3.

4.

5.

6.

7.

Preparations for Business Travel

The business traveler represents the organization. Some requirements placed on the traveler by the organization include the following:

1.

2.

3.

4.

In order to complete the itinerary it will be necessary to determine the exact travel needs. These needs will include both organizational requirements and personal preferences. Some of the personal preferences that the secretary must be aware of could include:

1.

2.

3.

4.

Name source books available for use if you are responsible for making travel arrangements.

Transportation guides

Hotel and motel indexes

Timetables

Atlases

Organizations have different ways to handle employee travel. Choices include:

1.

2.

3.

Services provided by a commercial travel agency include . . .

The traveler who uses the services of a commercial agency typically ( ) does ( ) does not pay the agency directly. With certain transportation reservations, the agency charges a flat services fee. For in-house services, operational costs may be charged to individual departments.

Confirmed transportation reservations will provide such information for the travel itinerary as:

1.

2.

3.

4.

5.

Information supplied by the secretary when making hotel or motel reservations may include:

1.

2.

3.

4.

5.

Information needed to reserve special types of facilities includes:

1.

2.

3.

4.

5.

6.

7.

8.

A trip file contains essential information and procedures involved in the business trip. A folder to be carried by the traveler might include:

1.

2.

3.

4.

Make statements about the commonly used types of travel funds listed below.

Traveler's checks

Letter of credit

Debit card

The **completed** itinerary includes the following types of information:

1.

2.

3.

4.

5.

6.

7.

Types of Travel

Domestic travel describes . . .

International travel describes . . .

Domestic transportation services available are:

1.

2.

3.

4.

and, selection of these services depends on:

1.

2.

3.

Air travel accommodations include:

1.

2.

3.

4.

National railway systems that connect metropolitan areas throughout the country are _____
and _____.

The _____ edition of **The Official Airline Guide** provides flight information for international air
transportation.

Foreign railway service offers both _____-class and _____-class train service.

An American International Driving Permit is available through the _____ _____
_____ **prior** to the trip. A United States driver's license is accepted in most countries.

Internationally, time is based on a 24-hour clock. Military time is also based on a 24-hour clock. Using
this format, how would you refer to . . .

3 a.m.?

11 a.m.?

6 p.m.?

Documents and Credentials

The difference between a **passport** and a **visa** is:

Passport

Visa

What is the procedure to follow when applying for a passport?

1.

2.

3.

4.

A passport is valid for _____ years.

In some instances inoculations, medications, or an Official International Certificate of Vaccination is required to travel in foreign countries. The purpose of an Official International Certificate of Vaccination is . . .

The Administrative Assistant's Role in Executive's Absence

Planning and confirming travel arrangements represents only half of the preparation. Other details to consider are:

1.

2.

3.

Follow-Up Activities

Follow-up activities should be completed as soon as possible. Such activities may include:

1.

2.

3.

4.

5.

CHAPTER 8: BUSINESS TRAVEL

Terms and Definitions

Use this page to record terms and definitions on which you want to concentrate, or to record additional information you have located from other resources.

CHAPTER 8: BUSINESS TRAVEL

Additional Comments

Use this page to record information found in readings, notes from lectures, or notes to yourself about topics to be researched.

CHAPTER 8: BUSINESS TRAVEL

Additional Comments

CHAPTER 9: RECORDS MANAGEMENT PRINCIPLES

Records Management is defined as the systematic control of recorded information required for the operation of an organization through the stages of creation, use, storage, transfer, and disposition. Records management incorporates both conventional and nonconventional documents. The management of records has become an extremely important office support function.

Analyzing Records and Records Systems

Define the two kinds of documents found in any business organization.

Records

Nonrecords

Records are classified by either:

1.

2.

Active records are . . .

Inactive records are . . .

Define and give examples of the four categories of records according to importance:

Vital

Important

Useful

Nonessential

Indicate the steps of the **records cycle** on the diagram below.

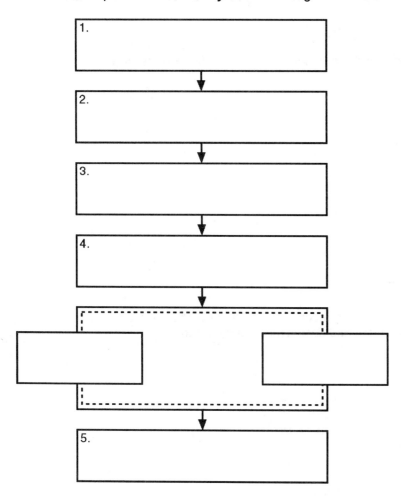

Basic considerations in the creation of new records should include:

1.

2.

3.

4.

5.

6.

7.

A records retention schedule estimates the period of time each type of record is to be held in active, semi-active, or inactive office storage.

In the process of establishing retention schedules, records are also evaluated in terms of:

1.

2.

3.

4.

"Purging" is the process of . . .

Records Creation, Design, and Control

The design of a record enhances the ability of the records manager to control the use of that record within the organization. Control in the creation and design function results in:

1.

2.

3.

4.

The two types of communication referred to as correspondence are:

1.

2.

A **business form** is a record that . . .

Two ways to classify business forms are:

1.

2.

The physical construction of a business form includes such things as:

1.

2.

3.

Give examples of:

Manual forms

Automated forms

The most expensive type of record within an organization tends to be the _____.

Why?

A **formal report** would most likely include the following sections:

1.

2.

3.

4.

5.

6.

7.

8.

Costs incurred as a result of preparing a business report include:

1.

2.

3.

4.

5.

6.

The two primary uses for **card** systems are:

1.

2.

A **relative index** is used for files using a _____ or _____ classification system.

Index records contain only _____ information.

In addition to correspondence, business forms, reports, and cards, other types of conventional records include:

1.

2.

3.

4.

5.

6.

Nonconventional records must be stored and cared for as carefully as conventional, or paper, documents. Microforms are a major classification of nonconventional formats. Examples of nonconventional records are listed below. Make statements about each of them:

Microforms

Audiovisual media

Electronic media

Examples of audiovisual media are:

1.

2.

3.

4.

5.

6.

7.

8.

A _____ is an electronic method of organizing facts and data in one or more computer data files. Define the following terms associated with this method.

Data

Field

Record

File

DBMS =

Key factors in developing a forms management program include:

1.

2.

3.

_____ _____ is one of the most important elements of a total records management program.

Filing Procedures for Manual and Automated Systems

Define the following terms:

Direct-access filing system

Indirect-access filing system

Inspecting a record

Indexing a record

Coding a record

Why is a record charge-out system important?

The security of electronically filed documents may include the use of:

1.

2.

The three primary classification systems for filing are:

1.

2.

3.

The oldest filing classification system is the _____ system.

The only direct filing system is the _____ system.

Explain the following numeric filing systems:

Straight-numeric

Duplex-numeric

Block codes

Middle-digit

Terminal-digit

Decimal numeric

Coded numeric

Chronological

The _____ and _____ filing classification systems use the alphabetic system as a base.

Some of the main concerns to be considered in selecting records storage equipment are:

1.

2.

3.

4.

5.

Define the following identification aids needed for paper document storage systems:

Guides

Primary guides

Secondary guides

Out guide

File folder

Color coding

The value of records depends upon the utilization of the records in ongoing operations. Define the following terms associated with record values.

Primary value

Administrative value

Legal value

Fiscal value

Research value

Secondary value

Information value

Evidence value

Records may be transferred from active to inactive status. Two transfer methods are:

1.

2.

Destruction methods for paper records include:

1.

2.

3.

Destruction methods for microform and magnetic records include:

1.

2.

3.

Most organizations are now recycling paper, cardboard, and shredded or pulverized paper.

Dispersal is a term used to indicate . . .

A business **archive** is . . .

Archives are maintained by organizations to:

1.

2.

3.

CHAPTER 9: RECORDS MANAGEMENT PRINCIPLES

Terms and Definitions

Use this page to record terms and definitions you want to concentrate on, or to record additional information you have located from other resources.

CHAPTER 9: RECORDS MANAGEMENT PRINCIPLES

Additional Comments

Use this page to record information found in readings, notes from lectures, or notes to yourself about information to be researched.

CHAPTER 9: RECORDS MANAGEMENT PRINCIPLES

Additional Comments

CHAPTER 10: REFERENCE MATERIALS

Knowing where to find information is an essential skill. The use of reference sources and resources is an effective tool in managing time and maintaining accurate information. Information-gathering techniques and an understanding of research are necessary for the executive secretary and administrative assistant.

Research Procedures

Guidelines for developing a set of procedures for researching business information include:

1.

2.

3.

4.

5.

List the kinds of information recorded in preparing a bibliography.

1.

2.

3.

4.

5.

6.

7.

8.

Research Facilities

Name places or groups of people where and with whom research might be conducted.

Places

Groups of people

Reference Materials

Enter the source of the information in Column B for the people, places, and things listed in Column A:

COLUMN A   **COLUMN B**

1. Manufacturers: products, locations   1.

2. Factual information about annual events   2.

3. Debate transcripts from Congress and the Senate   3.

4. Bibliographical information for corporations and executives   4.

5. Information about business etiquette   5.

6. Monthly information about bond issues and market positions 6.

7. Achievements of noted individuals   7.

8. An appropriate quotation for a speech   8.

9. Subject index of periodicals covering business-related topics 9.

10. Information about parliamentary procedures   10.

11. International mail regulations   11.

12. How to select lodging for a business trip   12.

13. Spelling and syllabification of words   13.

14. News item in a back issue of the **Wall Street Journal**   14.

15. Summary report about selected stocks, dividends, and earnings 15.

The **difference** between a **dictionary** and an **encyclopedia** is:

Evaluating Information References

Guidelines for evaluating information references include:

1.

2.

3.

4.

CHAPTER 10: REFERENCE MATERIALS

Terms and Definitions

Use this page to record terms and definitions you want to concentrate on, or to record additional information you have located from other resources.

CHAPTER 10: REFERENCE MATERIALS

Additional Comments

Use this page to record information found in readings, notes from lectures, or notes to yourself about information to be researched.

CHAPTER 10: REFERENCE MATERIALS

Additional Comments

CHAPTER 11: CONFERENCES AND MEETINGS

Many administrative assistants and executive secretaries are responsible for arranging meetings and conferences. The nature, location, and formality of the meeting, conference, or event will dictate the degree of preparation and involvement necessary. Checklists are helpful in conference and convention preparation.

Conferences

A **conference** is defined as . . .

Two types of conferences are:

1.

2.

Typical activities that need to be accomplished before, during, and after the conference include:

Before:
1.

2.

3.

4.

5.

6.

7.

8.

9.

10.

11.

12.

13.

14.

15.

16.

17.

18.

During:

1.

2.

3.

4.

5.

6.

7.

8.

After:

1.

2.

3.

4.

5.

6.

7.

Meetings

It is estimated that managers spend approximately _____ of their time in meetings each week.

Meetings tend to be organized either as _____ meetings or _____ meetings.

Define the **two** types of committees for planning and organizing meetings and special functions.

Standing

Ad hoc

Electronic media have introduced a new dimension to the meeting concept. Describe the following:

Teleconference

Videoconference

Computer conference

Data conference

An **agenda** is . . .

The usual order of business to be discussed or presented during a meeting is:

1.

2.

3.

4.

5.

6.

7.

8.

9.

10.

11.

12.

13.

14.

Parliamentary procedure has often been defined as "common sense used in a gracious manner." Basic principles of parliamentary procedure are:

1.

2.

3.

4.

Enacting parliamentary procedure calls for items of business to be presented during a meeting for action by the group in the form of a **motion**. Define the following types of motions.

Main motion

Subsidiary motion

Incidental motion

Privileged motion

Unclassified motion

A **quorum** is . . .

Typical kinds of visuals representing types of media other than paper used in meeting presentations are:

1.

2.

3.

The difference between a **resolution** and a **petition** is:

Resolution

Petition

Minutes are the official record of the meeting. The **purpose** of minutes is:

The preliminary draft of the minutes should be approved by the presiding officer (   ) before   (   ) after it is finalized and duplicated for distribution to the other members of the executive board or committee.

CHAPTER 11: CONFERENCES AND MEETINGS

Terms and Definitions

Use this page to record terms and definitions you want to concentrate on, or to record additional information you have located from other resources.

CHAPTER 11: CONFERENCES AND MEETINGS

Additional Comments

Use this page to record information found in readings, notes from lectures, or notes to yourself about information to be researched.

CHAPTER 11: CONFERENCES AND MEETINGS

Additional Comments

CHAPTER 12: REPROGRAPHICS MANAGEMENT

Reprographic processes represent a bulk of budget expenditures. Mentally review the numbers of reproductions made in your office. Effectiveness depends upon equipment selection, availability of well trained operators, and accuracy in the design and completion of office documents.

Reprographics is the office system with primary responsibility for preparing copies of documents needed during the operation of the organization. Reprographics may be divided into the following processes.

1.

2.

3.

4.

5.

6.

Determining Reprographic Needs

The criteria for selecting the best type of reprographic service needs include the following factors:

1.

2.

3.

4.

5.

Organizing Reprographic Systems

There are advantages and disadvantages to centralized/decentralized locations for reprographic equipment. Describe them.

Decentralized

Advantages

Disadvantages

Centralized

Advantages

Disadvantages

Some of the specific applications for in-house services include:

1.

2.

3.

4.

Controlling Reprographic Systems

Considerations when selecting reprographic equipment include:

1.

2.

3.

4.

5.

When matching production with a production process, considerations are:

1.

2.

3.

4.

Operation controls that might be used for reprographic services are:

1.

2.

3.

4.

5.

The primary cost factors in reprographic operations include:

1.

2.

3.

4.

"Hidden" costs in reprographic operations include:

1.

2.

3.

4.

Innovations and Trends in Reprographic Systems

Technology is permitting the creation of higher quality paper documents. Technology also allows high-speed production in less time. Innovations and trends in the office system include:

1.

2.

3.

4.

5.

6.

7.

CHAPTER 12: REPROGRAPHICS MANAGEMENT

Terms and Definitions

Use this page to record terms and definitions you want to concentrate on, or to record additional information you have located from other resources.

CHAPTER 12: REPROGRAPHICS MANAGEMENT

Additional Comments

Use this page to record information found in readings, notes from lectures, or notes to yourself about information to be researched.

CHAPTER 12: REPROGRAPHICS MANAGEMENT

Additional Comments

CHAPTER 13: INFORMATION DISTRIBUTION

Information is a critical element in today's society. Organizations are more conscious now than ever before about the importance of activities and timely communication--internal and external, manual and electronic.

Basic Principles of Information Distribution

Guidelines for implementing approximate means of information distribution include:

1.

2.

3.

4.

5.

Selecting approximate methods to use in distributing information requires the following considerations:

1.

2.

3.

4.

5.

Internal Information Distribution

Internal information distribution may include the following types:

1.

2.

3.

4.

External Information Distribution

Mail services, delivery services, and telecommunications are the primary means of . . .

Contents of envelopes from incoming mail should be checked for . . .

Name and differentiate the categories of outgoing mail as classified by the U.S. Postal Services:

1.

2.

3.

4.

5.

6.

7.

8.

A **certificate of mailing** is . . .

Explain the difference between registered mail and insured mail.

Postage for mail (letters and postal cards) going to Mexico ( ) is ( ) is not the same as that for letters and cards mailed within the United States.

The most prevalent users of the Internet are _____ and _____.

The primary reasons for electronic communication are:

1.

2.

3.

A service to transmit messages to foreign countries via telephone lines, fiber optic cables, microwave disks, or space satellites is _____ received through _____ _____.

Excellent reminders for telephone courtesy and efficiency are:

1.

2.

3.

4.

5.

Some advantages of using FAX transmissions are . . .

Etiquette practices for the electronic environment are often referred to as _____.

The home page is the _____ page of a Web site. A Web site consists of _____ of the pages collectively for an individual or company.

CHAPTER 13: INFORMATION DISTRIBUTION

Terms and Definitions

Use this page to record terms and definitions on which you want to concentrate, or to record additional information you have located from other resources.

CHAPTER 13: INFORMATION DISTRIBUTION

Additional Comments

Use this page to record information found in readings, notes from lectures, or notes to yourself about topics to be researched.

CHAPTER 13: INFORMATION DISTRIBUTION

Additional Comments

CHAPTER 14: DOCUMENT PRODUCTION

Office professionals are required to make many important decisions during the document production process. These decisions reflect their skill with keyboarding, software applications, hardware, business protocol and the English language.

Receiving Input for Document Production

Document input is received in a variety of ways. Name the most common forms of receiving input:

1.

2.

3.

The most common and the slowest form of input is _____.

General instructions given at the beginning of any dictated document should include:

Initiating Document Production

Questions regarding hardware and software the secretary responds to before document production is begun include:

1.

2.

3.

4.

5.

Document Production

The types and number of characters that can be used in a file name are determined by . . .

If each file name within an application and stored on the same medium is not unique, the result is . . .

File management ( ) is ( ) is not as important as it is in a paper system.

The decision to print or copy multiple copies may be determined at least in part by . . .

For the most efficient document production, the document format ( ) should ( ) should not be set prior to keying in the text for the document.

Evaluation of Document Production

Individual production can be measured in terms of _____ _____ or _____ produced within a particular period of time.

In reference to document production, define the following terms:

Productive time

Unproductive time

CHAPTER 14: DOCUMENT PRODUCTION

Terms and Definitions

Use this page to record terms and definitions on which you want to concentrate, or to record additional information you have located from other resources.

CHAPTER 14: DOCUMENT PRODUCTION

Additional Comments

Use this page to record information found in readings, notes from lectures, or notes to yourself about topics to be researched.

CHAPTER 14: DOCUMENT PRODUCTION

Additional Comments

CHAPTER 15: GENERAL OFFICE PROCEDURES

Management is the ability to obtain desired results through the use of available and appropriate resources (human and material) of an organization and the efforts of the individuals involved. The success of every organizational activity will be directly related to the skills of the manager.

Planning

Planning is . . .

Name and define the primary types of planning activities:

1.

2.

3.

Strategic, tactical, and operational planning within an organization must network to show consistent and supportive sets of objectives for the entire organization.

Guidelines for prioritizing work include:

1.

2.

3.

4.

5.

One of the easiest ways to categorize tasks is first to group the tasks into three primary categories. These categories are:

Priority 1 =

Priority 2 =

Priority 3 =

Tasks need to be analyzed within each priority category in sequence from the most important to the least important.

Name two ways this might be accomplished.

1.

2.

Common time scheduling techniques used by secretaries are:

1.

2.

3.

4.

5.

6.

Office tools used to simplify various work assignments and speed production processes may include:

1.

2.

3.

4.

5.

148

When analyzing routine office tasks, one basic goal should be to . . .

One way to analyze time requests for specific tasks is to . . .

Three types of planning schedules useful in office work are:

1.

2.

3.

Communication—both vertical and horizontal—is very important in maintaining productive working relationships among office personnel. Give examples of each.

Vertical

Horizontal

Two-way communication with superiors involves:

1.

2.

3.

Job sharing is . . .

Cross training is . . .

Organizing

Organizing permits the office administration to . . .

Support personnel may be organized according to the following plans. Define each:

Centralization

Decentralization

Matrix

In order to analyze and prioritize work assignments, it is necessary to know:

The principles of scientific management applied to office work are:

1.

2.

3.

4.

5.

A **logging form** is used to . . .

Reviewing task assignments before completing a job or assigning it to someone else for completion should include . . .

Policy and procedures are critical to office efficiency and effectiveness. Define the various types of office manuals listed below:

Organizational manual

Policy manual

Employee manual or handbook

Procedures or operations manual

Specialty guide or handbook

Supervising

Two functions are particularly unique to the supervision of office personnel. These are:

1.

2.

Staffing involves the following activities:

1.

2.

3.

4.

5.

6.

7.

Controlling involves the following two primary activities:

1.

2.

A **performance appraisal** is . . .

Primary considerations in implementing a performance appraisal system are:

1.

2.

3.

4.

Name and give examples of the three primary groups of performance appraisal methods.

1.

2.

3.

The purposes of the performance appraisal interview are:

1.

2.

3.

CHAPTER 15: GENERAL OFFICE PROCEDURES

Terms and Definitions

Use this page to record terms and definitions you want to concentrate on, or to record additional information you have located from other resources.

CHAPTER 15: GENERAL OFFICE PROCEDURES

Additional Comments

Use this page to record information found in readings, notes from lectures, or notes to yourself about information to be researched.

CHAPTER 15: GENERAL OFFICE PROCEDURES

Additional Comments

SECTION III: BUSINESS COMMUNICATION
CHAPTER 16: COMPOSING WRITTEN COMMUNICATIONS

Effective communication is the strength of a successful business. Communication skills—written, verbal, nonverbal, listening, and feedback—represent the tools necessary to build bridges instead of barriers whether the communication is one-on-one or group.

Fundamentals of Writing

Letters, reports, memos, telephone messages, instructions, and other written documentation depend upon the ability of the writer to express something on paper. The writer focuses upon a mental image of the reader in selecting:

• words (connotation and denotation); and

• examples, illustrations

The key to effective word selection is to use:

1.

2.

3.

Messages should be . . .

Tone is defined as . . .

Tone, together with _____, form the overall impression for the reader.

Words precise in meaning are examples of ( ) concrete ( ) abstract language.

The more effective business writing tone is . . .

Words where meanings can be interpreted differently by different people, even in the same situation, are examples of ( ) concrete ( ) abstract language.

_____are used to describe nouns or subjects and to support active verbs.

_____modify verbs, adjectives, or other adverbs.

Points to help improve the quality of sentences and paragraphs include:

1.

2.

Sentences should normally average from _____ to _____ words.

A paragraph has one main idea presented and may be written in the _____ or _____ style.

Sentences and paragraphs need to be constructed with several qualities, which may include:

1.

2.

3.

4.

5.

6.

7.

List ways to show emphasis in written documents:

1.

2.

3.

4.

Sex-fair language is also a consideration. Language in business writing must be free of sexual bias. Change the words listed below to asexual terms.

saleslady   =

mailman   =

delivery man   =

manhours   =

"man the booth"   =

male secretary   =

the ladies and the men   =

man and wife   =

female executive   =

Name three ways changes in word usage can be achieved to take into account sex-fair language.

1.

2.

3.

The identification of racial or ethnic origin should likewise not appear in writing unless it is pertinent to the message being conveyed.

Communication that will create goodwill needs to express consideration for the other person. Goodwill may be created through:

1.

2.

3.

4.

5.

159

Business Letters

Business letters have three basic formats—**positive, neutral, negative.** Give significant points about the paragraph formation of each of these letter types (opening, body, closing).

Positive (direct, deductive):

Neutral:

Negative (indirect, inductive):

The combination letter contains both a _____ and _____ response.

Persuasive letters have a special formula. Complete the formula. Define what each letter in the acronym means.

A

I

D

160

A **form** letter is correspondence with some identical parts. The three types of form letters are:

1.

2.

3.

The wording that will stay exactly the same on every letter produced is _____ information.

_____ information is any text that must be inserted to complete the message. This information will change on each letter produced.

Two methods that are used in word processing for the preparation of letters with variable information include the use of:

1.

2.

Memoranda within the Organization

The most common form of communication within an organization is through interoffice communication. Interoffice communication takes the form of _____ or short, informal _____.

Interoffice means from one office to another within an organization. _____ means from one organization to another.

Memoranda, just as with business letters, can be prepared that are:

1.

2.

3.

The informal or short report is another form of interoffice communication. Types of informal or short reports are:

1.

2.

3.

Electronic Mail

Some of the advantages of e-mail are:

-

-

-

-

Business Reports

There are six report classifications. Explain each category.

Material

-

-

Time interval

-

-

-

Information flow

-

-

-

-

Context

-

-

Function

-

-

Message style

-

-

-

The **report** is the product of research—primary and secondary. In planning and designing research the problem must be defined before the subsequent steps in the process may be pursued directly. The rest of the report format depends upon the data collected. Data collection is conducted through:

Secondary research (define and make statements about this type)

Primary research (define and make statements about this type)

Define and make statements about each method of data collection listed below:

Mail questionnaire

Personal interview

Telephone interview

Data are collected then organized, classified, edited, coded, tabulated, statistically analyzed, and evaluated. After each of these steps is performed, a report may be prepared according to universally acceptable procedures or organizationally established guidelines.

The final step in the research process is the writing of the report. A formal report may be subdivided into the following three primary sections. Name the three divisions and the features of each:

1.

-

-

-

-

-

-

2.

-

-

-

3.

-

-

-

-

Cross-Cultural Communication

Five strategies for dealing with cultural differences are:

1.

2.

3.

4.

5.

Cultural differences are embedded in the _____. All other human differences are embedded in _____.

The use of _____ is particularly important when communicating with people from a culture different from your own.

People of all cultures deserve our _____ and openness to differences.

It is only through collaborating that the communication produces information and knowledge, resulting in the best decision to benefit us all.

CHAPTER 16: COMPOSING WRITTEN COMMUNICATIONS

Terms and Definitions

Use this page to record terms and definitions you want to concentrate on, or to record additional information you have located from other resources.

CHAPTER 16: COMPOSING WRITTEN COMMUNICATIONS

Additional Comments

Use this page to record information found in readings, notes from lectures, or notes to yourself about information to be researched.

CHAPTER 16: COMPOSING WRITTEN COMMUNICATIONS

Additional Comments

CHAPTER 17: EDITING WRITTEN COMMUNICATIONS

Researching and composing are only part of the overall written communication process. Documents are prepared with the reader or receiver in mind. They must be presented with correctness, clarity, conciseness, coherence, and courtesy.

Proofreading

Proofreading is the process of checking final copy for spelling, punctuation, and formatting. Proofreading is necessary to be sure internal and external communications are purposeful and professional.

Explain the meaning of the following proofreader's symbols.

SYMBOL	MEANING
stet	
(transpose symbol)	
[	
(insert symbol)	
#	
(close up symbol)	

Material must be proofed both for _____ errors and for _____ .

Proofreading techniques include:

1.

2.

3.

4.

5.

Proofreading software includes a spell-check feature. The purpose of the spelling feature is to check the document for spelling errors.

Editing for Technical Correctness

Command of the English language entails using:

1.

2.

3.

4.

5.

Describe **conversational** English.

Formal English is characterized by . . .

For a sentence to be complete, it must contain a _____ and a _____.

The four components of a sentence are subject, verb, object, and complement.

Action verbs are usually followed by a _____ _____.

The language is further enhanced by appropriate formatting and consistent language style.

Punctuation is critical to intended messages. Punctuation can also be used to effect emphasis. Define the common uses and point of emphasis for each of the following marks.

' (apostrophe)

: (colon)

, (comma)

— (dash)

. . . (ellipses)

! (exclamation point)

- (hyphen)

( ) (parentheses)

. (period)

? (question mark)

"   " (quotation marks)

; (semicolon)

<u>underscore</u>

$ $ $ Sums of money are expressed as figures.

172

In legal copy, money is expressed in both _____ and _____.

Proper capitalization makes a written document appear neat and easier to read. Some of the most frequent uses of capitalization are:

1.

2.

3.

4.

5.

6.

7.

8.

9.

10.

11.

12.

13.

Document format provides the visual impact. The three most common **letter formats** are:

1.

2.

3.

General suggestions for word division are:

1.

2.

3.

4.

5.

6.

The purpose of grammar software is:

Copyediting for Application of Writing Fundamentals

Copyediting is . . .

Copyediting requires skill in the following areas:

1.

2.

3.

4.

5.

174

Tone is the manner in which the attitude is expressed. The majority of writing has the tone of:

1.

2.

3.

4.

Documents may be written in either a direct or indirect approach. The direct approach is sometimes referred to as the _____ approach. The indirect approach may also be referred to as the _____ approach.

What is the difference in these two approaches.

What is the purpose of the copyediting style sheet?

175

CHAPTER 17: EDITING WRITTEN COMMUNICATIONS

Terms and Definitions

Use this page to record terms and definitions you want to concentrate on, or to record additional information you have located from other resources.

CHAPTER 17: EDITING WRITTEN COMMUNICATIONS

Additional Comments

Use this page to record information found in readings, notes from lectures, or notes to yourself about information to be researched.

CHAPTER 17: EDITING WRITTEN COMMUNICATIONS

Additional Comments

CHAPTER 18: ABSTRACTING WRITTEN COMMUNICATIONS

To present information within the correct context materials are previewed and summarized. There are distinct differences in commenting on and reporting on the works of another person.

Techniques for Abstracting

Summarizing material requires practice. Explain each of the following techniques which an office professional may use.

Photocopying

Highlighting key points

Summarizing key points

Computerized searches

Fair uses of copyrighted materials include:

1.

2.

Yahoo is an example of a . . .

Effective Abstracts and Précis

Define and make statements about the following terms:

Abstract

Précis

Name the four writing characteristics that can be used as flags to identify key points of an original document.

1.

2.

3.

4.

A **précis** is always typed in _____ format.

Material is quoted verbatim in a (n)   (   ) précis   (   ) abstract.

Material is paraphrased in a (n) (   ) précis   (   ) abstract.

Identify the information that should be included in a bibliographic notation.

1.

2.

3.

4.

5.

6.

7.

8.

9.

CHAPTER 18: ABSTRACTING WRITTEN COMMUNICATIONS

Terms and Definitions

Use this page to record terms and definitions you want to concentrate on, or to record additional information you have located from other resources.

CHAPTER 18: ABSTRACTING WRITTEN COMMUNICATIONS

Additional Comments

Use this page to record information found in readings, notes from lectures, or notes to yourself about information to be researched.

CHAPTER 18: ABSTRACTING WRITTEN COMMUNICATIONS

Additional Comments

CHAPTER 19: PREPARING WRITTEN COMMUNICATIONS
IN FINAL FORMAT

The format used for preparing the business letter will help to create attractive, well-placed copy.

Business Letter Format

The parts of the business letter are:

1.

2.

3.

4.

5.

6.

7.

8.

9.

10.

11.

List the characteristics of each of the business letter styles shown below:

Block

Modified block

184

Simplified

All special notations (CONFIDENTIAL, PERSONAL, AIR-MAIL, CERTIFIED, REGISTERED, and SPECIAL DELIVERY) are typed a _____ space below the date line, at the _____ margin, and in all capital letters.

The two punctuation styles used in business writing today are:

1.

2.

The heading for the second page of a business letter should include:

1.

2.

3.

Envelopes

The U.S. Postal Service prefers that an envelope address be no longer than four lines. The U.S. Postal Service uses OCR (optical character recognition) equipment for scanning/sorting mail. Guidelines from the Postal Service request that information be in all caps with no punctuation; the two-letter state code and a five- or nine-digit Zip code must be included.

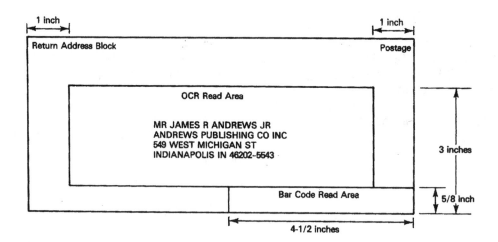

To conform to postal OCR requirements, all lines of an address on an envelope should be:

• typed in _____ _____ _____.

• typed with no _____.

• typed _____ spaced.

• typed and blocked at the _____.

These guidelines also apply to addresses placed on labels.

Memoranda Format

The four notation lines found in memo headings are:

1.

2.

3.

4.

Make one (or more) statement(s) about each of the following terms as they relate to a memo format.

Spacing

Notation line placement

Reference initials

Business Report Format

Reports can be prepared informally following a memorandum format or in a more formal format. Companies, agencies, or educational institutions usually have preferences about format. There are also published stylebooks to assist in report preparation. Make statements about considerations for:

Physical layout

Line spacing and paragraphing

Headings

Pagination

Automatic generation of supplements

Widow line

Reference notes or reference citations are used to . . .

Explain the differences between:

Footnote

Endnote

List the information included in a footnote or endnote entry:

Citations give proper credit for . . .

A **bibliography** is . . .

Name and define the three basic types of bibliographies:

1.

2.

3.

The format of a bibliography dictates its appearance by:

1.

2.

3.

The term **graphics** refers to . . .

A graphic aid is . . .

The five requirements for including a graphic illustration in a written report are:

1.

2.

3.

4.

5.

The basic types of graphic illustrations used to display detailed data are _____
and _____.

Place the following information appropriately on the pie chart below.

The percentages of candidates passing the individual sections of the CPS® examination are represented below:

53%   Office Administration/Communication
27%   Management
20%   Finance and Business Law

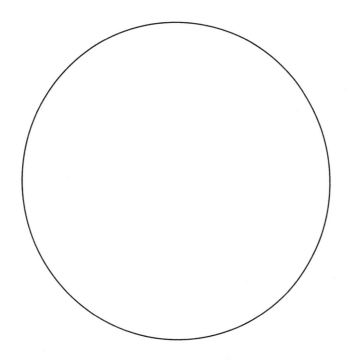

CPS® Examination Profile
An Example of a Pie Graph

Other Forms of Business Communications

Minutes

Secretaries are often given the responsibility of taking and transcribing notes about the events of a meeting. This information Is called the **Minutes of a Meeting**. Minutes become the official report of the meeting.

Organizations and associations may have forms prepared for recording minutes. Name the common pieces of information that should be included in minutes—both formal and informal meetings—and make statements about each.

1.

2.

3.

4.

5.

News Releases

Describe the considerations in preparing a **news release**:

Heading

Body

Closing symbols

Spacing

Outline

An **outline** consists of key words coded in descending order, using roman numerals, numbers, and letters of the alphabet.

Traditional outlines follow the **I, A-Z, 1, a-z, (I), (a)-(z)** format. Non-traditional outlines may take the shape of a mind map.

Itinerary

An **itinerary** is an executive's travel plan that specifies all details concerning business travel. The itinerary typically includes the following details:

1.

2.

3.

4.

5.

6.

Outlines for speeches may follow one of the types of format below. Describe each.

Topical

Phrase

Sentence

Speech

The basic steps in preparing a speech include:

1.

2.

3.

4.

CHAPTER 19: PREPARING WRITTEN COMMUNICATIONS
IN FORMAL FORMAT

Terms and Definitions

Use this page to record terms and definitions you want to concentrate on, or to record additional information you have located from other resources.

CHAPTER 19: PREPARING WRITTEN COMMUNICATIONS
IN FORMAL FORMAT

Additional Comments

Use this page to record information found in readings, notes from lectures, or notes to yourself about information to be researched.

CHAPTER 19: PREPARING WRITTEN COMMUNICATIONS
IN FORMAL FORMAT

Additional Comments

CHAPTER 20: ORAL COMMUNICATIONS

This chapter involves the major elements of oral communication, such as interpersonal communication, listening, nonverbal cues, and effective presentation skills. Communication affects us in every part of our lives. Ineffective communication is the cause of more conflict and dissatisfaction than any other one single behavior. It is critical to be aware of the elements of positive communication skills and to strive to practice them.

The Enhancement of Understanding

A working definition of **communication** is . . .

Speakers and listeners simultaneously send and receive messages. When you are not conversing with another, you are talking to _____.

Communication requires the attachment of some _____ to the message that has been sent or received. When you communicate, you transmit information both _____ and _____.

Insert the labels for the communication process model shown below.

Examples of the nonverbal aspects of communication are:

1.

2.

3.

The communication response, often referred to as _____, helps you to determine if the message you sent was truly received and understood.

Communication in the workplace is important for several reasons. Name these reasons.

1.

2.

3.

4.

5.

6.

7.

8.

The worst assumption anyone can make about a message just sent or received is that . . .

The six major factors in the communication process are:

1.

2.

3.

4.

5.

6.

The process of assigning and organizing symbols to formulate the message you want to send is called . . .

The symbols that you select as your message can be:

1.

2.

3.

The connecting device between the speaker and the listener through which the message is sent is the channel. Examples of communication channels are:

1.

2.

3.

4.

5.

6.

The examples of communication channels listed above will typically fall into two categories—**impersonal** and **direct personal**. Define each of these channel classifications and then label the example in the previous listing as to whether there are impersonal or direct personal.

The process by which the listener(s) interprets the meaning of the message is known as . . .

Feedback is the listener's response to the message. Two special problems may occur with feedback. Name and explain these potential problems.

Distractions interfere with effective communication. There are three basic categories of distractions. Give examples of these three types.

External

Internal

Semantic

Giving and Receiving Praise and Criticism

_____ is acknowledging the effective work of others. Guidelines for giving praise may include:

1.

2.

Criticism, when done properly, helps to enhance a person's abilities and to build him/her up. Explain the "sandwich" theory of giving criticism.

Guidelines for receiving criticism may include:

1.

2.

3.

Becoming a More Effective Listener

Most office personnel spend approximately 40 percent of their workday listening. The average person listens at a 25 percent efficiency level.

According to your text, the definition for listening is . . .

The first problem inherent in the listening process involves

The average person speaks at a rate of _____ wpm. The average listener can follow and understand information at a rate of _____ wpm. Research shows that the average person remembers only _____ percent of what he/she heard in the listening process.

Listening habits that studies show the average American might consider changing are:

1.

2.

3.

4.

5.

6.

7.

8.

Ways to show you are listening are:

1.

2.

3.

4.

5.

6.

7.

8.

Techniques for improving listening include:

1.

2.

3.

4.

Nonverbal Communication: Listening Between the Words

Research tells us that as much as 90 percent of the impact of messages is based on nonverbal aspects. Nonverbal communication is . . .

Body language, the most prominent element in nonverbal communication, refers to:

1.

2.

3.

4.

5.

When you are engaged in vocal communication, your voice quality adds variety and excitement. Name common characteristics of your voice:

1.

2.

3.

4.

5.

Space, distance, and touch are also examples of nonverbal communication. The most common form of touch in the business environment is the _____.

Time is also a communicator and tends to say something to others about your attitude and personality.

Name and make a statement about each of the four Cs (cues) of nonverbal communication:

1.

2.

3.

4.

Giving a Professional Presentation

When you prepare to write a speech, the following guidelines are helpful:

1.

2.

3.

4.

5.

6.

CHAPTER 20: ORAL COMMUNICATIONS

Terms and Definitions

Use this page to record terms and definitions you want to concentrate on, or to record additional information you have located from other resources.

CHAPTER 20: ORAL COMMUNICATIONS

Additional Comments

Use this page to record information found in readings, notes from lectures, or notes to yourself about information to be researched.

CHAPTER 20: ORAL COMMUNICATIONS

Additional Comments

NOTES

NOTES

NOTES

Study Tip Exam Prep (S.T.E.P.) Card
OFFICE TECHNOLOGY

Mentally review these terms until you can define them quickly.

1. byte
2. discrete media
3. brightness ratio
4. microprocessor
5. chat rooms
6. OCR
7. footcandle
8. menu
9. job analysis
10. compatibility
11. jacket
12. visual dysfunction
13. batch processing
14. CPU
15. ROM
16. biomechanics
17. WATS
18. merge
19. archive
20. word processing
21. soft copy
22. floppy disk
23. terminal
24. serial printer
25. feasibility study

26. World Wide Web
27. fluorescent
28. fiber optics
29. centralized system
30. euthenics
31. task light
32. buffer
33. ink jet
34. e-mail
35. hardware
36. white noise
37. laser
38. microcomputer
39. LAN
40. hard disk
41. integration
42. minicomputer
43. courier services
44. luminaire
45. ultrafiche
46. parallel
47. mainframe
48. microfiche
49. decibel
50. dedicated unit

51. computer system
52. modem
53. peripherals
54. ergonomics
55. keyboard
56. monitor
57. cybernetics
58. printer
59. operating system
60. database
61. storage media
62. shared logic
63. flow chart
64. call directory
65. video disk technology
66. voice storage
67. integrated software
68. nonvolatile storage
69. light pen
70. micrographics
71. delete
72. office landscaping
73. hard copy
74. BASIC
75. font

76. output
77. absorption
78. binary code
79. digital signals
80. incandescent
81. workstation
82. microfilm
83. record
84. sort
85. cool colors
86. work flow
87. 911
88. electronic blackboard
89. traditional office design
90. cassette
91. MIS
92. pagination
93. impact printer
94. machine language
95. teleconference
96. global search
97. formatting
98. telecommunications
99. centrex system
100. ambient lighting

Study Tip Exam Prep (S.T.E.P.) Card
OFFICE TECHNOLOGY

Mentally review these terms until you can define them quickly.

1. byte
2. discrete media
3. brightness ratio
4. microprocessor
5. chat rooms
6. OCR
7. footcandle
8. menu
9. job analysis
10. compatibility
11. jacket
12. visual dysfunction
13. batch processing
14. CPU
15. ROM
16. biomechanics
17. WATS
10. merge
19. archive
20. word processing
21. soft copy
22. floppy disk
23. terminal
24. serial printer
25. feasibility study

26. World Wide Web
27. fluorescent
28. fiber optics
29. centralized system
30. euthenics
31. task light
32. buffer
33. ink jet
34. e-mail
35. hardware
36. white noise
37. laser
38. microcomputer
39. LAN
40. hard disk
41. integration
42. minicomputer
43. courier services
44. luminaire
45. ultrafiche
46. parallel
47. mainframe
48. microfiche
49. decibel
50. dedicated unit

51. computer system
52. modem
53. peripherals
54. ergonomics
55. keyboard
56. monitor
57. cybernetics
58. printer
59. operating system
60. database
61. storage media
62. shared logic
63. flow chart
64. call directory
65. video disk technology
66. voice storage
67. integrated software
68. nonvolatile storage
69. light pen
70. micrographics
71. delete
72. office landscaping
73. hard copy
74. BASIC
75. font

76. output
77. absorption
78. binary code
79. digital signals
80. incandescent
81. workstation
82. microfilm
83. record
84. sort
85. cool colors
86. work flow
87. 911
88. electronic blackboard
89. traditional office design
90. cassette
91. MIS
92. pagination
93. impact printer
94. machine language
95. teleconference
96. global search
97. formatting
98. telecommunications
99. centrex system
100. ambient lighting

1

FIBER OPTICS

2

MAGNETIC MEDIA

3

MODEM

4

INK JET

5

FORTRAN

6

LAN

2

1. An input/output storage device.
2. Types of magnetic media include:
   - Magnetic tape (tape drives)
   - Magnetic disks (disk pack)
   - Floppy disks (flexible platter)
3. Magnetic tape is one of the most common media for input and secondary storage.

1

1. Method of information transmission
2. Data is converted by a laser to light signals along fine glass threads.
3. The conversion from sound to light waves has improved speed and accuracy of transmission.

4

1. A non-impact printer
2. Prints bi-directionally
3. Sprays ink on the page in two passes

3

1. May be internal or external to the computer system.
2. Converts digital signals to analog signals.
3. Transmission requires compatible modem at the point of origination and destination.

6

1. Local area networks allow transmission of data between systems within a building or among buildings of very limited geographical area.
2. Networking provides a sharing of resources.
3. Network configurations include:
   a. Star   b. Ring   c. Bus

5

1. A computer language.
2. Termed a third-generation language.
3. Must be converted into machine (binary) language that the computer can read.
4. Typically used when writing scientific, as opposed to business, programs.

7

RING NETWORK CONFIGURATION

8

STAR NETWORK CONFIGURATION

9

BUS NETWORK CONFIGURATION

10

MAIN MEMORY

11

TYPES OF COMPUTER SYSTEMS

12

PHOTOCOMPOSITION

1. All components are connected to a central controller.
2. Entire network is inoperable if the central controller malfunctions.
3. Star networks are cost efficient and can accommodate both voice and data.

1. Information passes unidirectionally toward destination.
2. Most systems permit only one message at a time.
3. There is no central controller.
4. Ring networks do not allow the integration of voice, data, and video on the same system.

1. Primary storage is another term for main memory.
2. Main memory stores: input, program, instructions, intermediate processing, results and output data.
3. Information must be in the main memory to be sent to the outgoing device or peripheral equipment.

1. A single, bi-directional communication link.
2. The most popular design.
3. When one component is inoperable, the network usually will not go down.
4. Only one message may be transmitted at a time.

1. A process where characters are printed optically onto photosensitive paper.
2. This process allows a variety of style and sizes of style and sizes of type on-line.
3. Word processors are one means of input into photocopiers.

The three categories of computer systems are:
1. Mainframe
2. Minicomputer
3. Microcomputer

13

PLOTTER

14

ROTARY FILES

15

APPLICATION SOFTWARE

16

REPROGRAPHIC FINISHING
PROCESSES

17

OPTICAL DISK
STORAGE

18

ADMINISTRATIVE SUPPORT

14

1. A mechanized system that rotates around a hub.
2. The file may be in the form of shelves, tubs, hanging folders, or card trays that move to the user.
3. Automated rotary files, at the touch of a button, locate records and move them to the operator.

13

1. Special type of printer.
2. Outlines drawings using a stylus.
3. Both diagonal as well as vertical and horizontal output is possible.

16

Common processes:
1. Collating
2. Stapling
3. Stitching
4. Binding
5. Folding

15

1. Application programs for specific tasks.
2. Programs include word processing, payroll operations, spreadsheet, database, and inventory operations, among others.

18

Tasks and responsibilities pertaining to office procedures that do not involve typing, most often, but do involve such responsibilities as telephoning, filing, arranging appointments, and receiving visitors.

17

1. Storage medium resembling a phonograph record.
2. Data is stored and retrieved with a laser.
3. Three types of optical disks are available:
    a. Optical videodisk
    b. Compact disk
    c. Optical digital data disk.

19

EXTERNAL ENVIRONMENT

20

INTELLIGENT COPIER
PRINTER

21

FAX

22

FLOPPY DISK

23

SECONDARY STORAGE

24

BUBBLE MEMORY

20

1. Integrates computer technology with other automated systems (WP and DP).
2. Prints hard copy from electronic signals.
3. Input from multiple workstations can be integrated to produce output.

19

Include:

Lighting	Static electricity
Color	Power
Sound	Security
Air	Energy conservation
Surfaces	

22

1. A storage medium
2. Available in two sizes: 3-1/2 and 5-1/4.

21

Facsimile Imaging
1. FAX imaging may be used in transmission or scanning.
2. Text, drawings, charts, and maps are among the materials that can be transmitted by FAX.
3. Machine to machine communication.

24

1. Magnetized spots on a thin layer of semiconductor material.
2. Can hold 92,000 bits of data on a 1-inch square chip.
3. High reliability because there are no moving parts.

23

1. Storage that is separate from the CPU.
2. Provides the capability of processing larger quantities of data.
3. Stores data in a format compatible with the data stored in primary storage.

25

RAM

26

ROM

27

ENDLESS LOOP

28

TIME-SHARE SYSTEMS

29

CALL DIRECTOR

30

CENTREX

26

1. Read only memory
2. Permanent memory
3. Stores for recorded programs or functions.
4. Cannot be changed by programming instructions.

25

1. Random access memory
2. Temporary memory
3. Stores programs and data that can be changed during the processing period.

28

1. WP/DP services purchased from service bureaus.
2. Data is input at the client's office.

27

1. Centralized recording/dictation system
2. Offers simultaneous recording and transcription.
3. The recording tape is encased in a tank.

30

1. A telephone system
2. Each station is connected separately to the central office.
3. Calls are transferred directly to the station called without going through a PBX operator.

29

1. Desktop telephone unit.
2. Handles a maximum of 29 lines at one location.
3. Can be connected to a switchboard or intercom system.

Mentally review these terms until you can define them quickly.

1. visa
2. organizing
3. archives
4. passport
5. mailgram
6. reprographics
7. questionnaire
8. MBO
9. system
10. traveler's check
11. almanac
12. Telex
13. decentralization
14. indexing
15. format
16. copyright
17. webmaster
18. file name
19. microforms
20. Standard and Poor's
21. chronological files
22. travel advance
23. parallelism
24. vital records
25. endnote

26. Official Airline Guide (OAG)
27. URL
28. documentation
29. travel agencies
30. videoconference
31. dispersal
32. Ayer's Directory
33. 24-hour clock
34. active records
35. input
36. third-class mail
37. turnaround time
38. centralization
39. Official Guide of Railways
40. subsidiary motion
41. blocked letter style
42. privileged motion
43. primary research
44. domestic travel
45. positive letter
46. Internet
47. secondary research
48. perpetual transfer
49. source books
50. work measurement

51. agenda
52. file folder
53. policy manual
54. periodic file transfer
55. aperture card
56. netiquette
57. motion
58. editing
59. jargon
60. primary guide
61. jacket
62. OCR
63. petition
64. international travel
65. ad hoc committee
66. conciseness
67. abstract
68. bibliography
69. Auditron
70. buffer
71. matrix plan
72. trip file
73. quorum
74. conference/convention
75. proofreading

76. static information
77. horizontal communication
78. vertical communication
79. operations manual
80. trip folder
81. copyright laws
82. procedures manual
83. minutes
84. external communication
85. records management
86. debit card
87. important records
88. Thomas' register
89. computer databank
90. Robert's Rules of Order
91. paragraph heading
92. electronic blackboard
93. standing committee
94. McRae's Blue Book
95. variable information
96. simplified letter style
97. nonessential records
98. editing software
99. vertical report
100. charge-out cards

Study Tip Exam Prep (S.T.E.P.) Card
OFFICE ADMINISTRATION AND COMMUNICATION

Mentally review these terms until you can define them quickly.

1. visa
2. organizing
3. archives
4. passport
5. mailgram
6. reprographics
7. questionnaire
8. MBO
9. system
10. traveler's check
11. almanac
12. Telex
13. decentralization
14. indexing
15. format
16. copyright
17. webmaster
18. file name
19. microforms
20. Standard and Poor's
21. chronological files
22. travel advance
23. parallelism
24. vital records
25. endnote

26. Official Airline Guide (OAG)
27. URL
28. documentation
29. travel agencies
30. videoconference
31. dispersal
32. Ayer's Directory
33. 24-hour clock
34. active records
35. input
36. third-class mail
37. turnaround time
38. centralization
39. Official Guide of Railways
40. subsidiary motion
41. blocked letter style
42. privileged motion
43. primary research
44. domestic travel
45. positive letter
46. Internet
47. secondary research
48. perpetual transfer
49. source books
50. work measurement

51. agenda
52. file folder
53. policy manual
54. periodic file transfer
55. aperture card
56. netiquette
57. motion
58. editing
59. jargon
60. primary guide
61. jacket
62. OCR
63. petition
64. international travel
65. ad hoc committee
66. conciseness
67. abstract
68. bibliography
69. Auditron
70. buffer
71. matrix plan
72. trip file
73. quorum
74. conference/convention
75. proofreading

76. static information
77. horizontal communication
78. vertical communication
79. operations manual
80. trip folder
81. copyright laws
82. procedures manual
83. minutes
84. external communication
85. records management
86. debit card
87. important records
88. Thomas' register
89. computer databank
90. Robert's Rules of Order
91. paragraph heading
92. electronic blackboard
93. standing committee
94. McRae's Blue Book
95. variable information
96. simplified letter style
97. nonessential records
98. editing software
99. vertical report
100. charge-out cards

1

POSITIVE LETTER

2

OFFICIAL AIRLINE GUIDE

3

DATABASE

4

PASSPORT

5

EDITOR'S
PROOFREADING SYMBOLS

6

NUMERIC FILING PLAN

2

A subscription service which is available in printed or automated form. One of several publications: OAG Pocket Flight Guide; OAG Worldwide Edition; OAG Desktop Flight Guide. Subscribers receive updates. INFORMATION: airline, time zone of destination city; airports accessible and their abbreviation; flight arrival and departure time, fares, aircraft, class available, days of flight operation.

1

A positive letter presents good news to the reader. A positive letter is written in the deductive (direct) approach. A positive letter ends with a note of goodwill.

4

Issued by Department of State. Official document granting permission to a specified individual to travel to a foreign country. Passport should be signed as soon as received. During travel, a passport should always be carried on the person and never left in a room or luggage. Report loss of a passport to the nearest passport office or, if abroad, to the nearest consulate.

3

A database is an electronic method of organizing facts or data that involves the creation of one or more computer data files.

6

The numeric filing plan is the most confidential of filing classifications. Requires alphabetic card index as an indirect filing system. Contains miscellaneous alphabetic file for correspondence.

5

Examples of proofreading symbols:

∿ transpose   ⋏ insert

↗ delete   ⋏ insert comma

≡ capitalize   ℓc lower case

⌒ close up space   check spelling

  add space

7

NEWS RELEASE

8

ELEMENTS OF A SYSTEM

9

ORGANIZATIONAL MANUAL

10

EMPLOYEE MANUAL

11

RECORD CYCLE

12

VITAL RECORD

- People
- Process (technology)
- Procedures

Considerations when preparing a news release include:
1. Release date
2. Contact person—preferably two—and how to reach them,
3. Title or subject focus
4. Double-space body
5. Number pages
6. Type "--more--" at bottom of all but last page
7. Type # # # to indicate end of release

An employee manual contains such information as:
1. Work hours
2. Dress code
3. Savings plan
4. Health insurance plan
5. Tuition reimbursement policy
6. Reporting sickness
7. Vacation plan
8. Retirement plan
9. Grievance procedure

An organizational manual contains such information as:
1. Relationships of divisions/departments (organization chart)
2. Mission statement
3. Historical information
4. Duties and responsibilities by division/department
5. Other information may be added relating to objectives.

Vital records are essential for the effective continuous operation of a firm. Examples:
1. Property deeds
2. Franchises
3. Birth certificates
4. Copyrights
5. Legal documents
6. Accounts receivable

A record cycle consists of the following steps:
1. Creation
2. Use
3. Storage
4. Transfer
5. Disposal

13

ULTRAFICHE

14

MICROFILM

15

JACKET

16

MIDDLE-DIGIT
FILING SYSTEM
48-23-11

17

TELECONFERENCE

18

MAIN MOTION

14

Characteristics of a microfilm:
1. Oldest type of microform.
2. Stores page images side by side on roll of film.
3. Available rolls are a standard 100 feet.
4. Stores up to 2500 letter-size images.

13

Characteristics of an ultrafiche:
1. Microform
2. 4 x 6 sheet of film
3. Read from left to right
4. Read from top to bottom
5. Contains hundreds of microimages

16

A numeric system that uses the middle digits of a number as the primary indexing units.

                    Primary
                    (drawer)
        48   -   23   -   11
    Secondary   Tertiary
      (guide)   (folder)

15

Characteristics of a jacket:
1. Microform.
2. Most convenient microform for making changes or updates.
3. Plastic unitized record.
4. 4 x 6

18

A main motion:
1. States an item of business.
2. Has the lowest precedence in rank among motions.
3. Must be seconded and is subject to discussion, debate, and amendment.

17

Characteristics of a teleconference are
1. "Meeting" through telephone communications with people in different locations.
2. Factor in time management and budget controls.
3. Also called audioconference—only uses sound, not sight.
4. Must be scheduled before the meeting date.

19

VIDEOCONFERENCE

20

PRIVILEGED MOTION

21

PARLIAMENTARY PROCEDURE

22

TRANSPARENCY

23

PETITION

24

ELECTRONIC BLACKBOARDS

20

A privileged motion:
1. Has the highest order of precedence.
2. Affects the comfort of the group.
3. Is referred to as the "convenience motion."

19

A videoconference is a meeting where:
1. Participants view each other on closed-circuit TV.
2. Freeze-frame can be used to emphasize or review certain materials.
3. Electronic blackboard, facsimile, or intelligent copiers are often used.

22

A transparency is an acetate sheet that contains an image burned or drawn on it that can be projected on a screen.

Transparencies can be prepared on various types of copiers.

Transparencies come in colored background or print.

21

Parliamentary procedure is a set of rules established for the appropriate conduct of business meetings.

24

A device used in conjunction with teleconferences or videoconferences.

COMPONENTS:
Location 1:
- Pressure-sensitive blackboard
- Microphone and speaker

Location 2:
- TV monitor
- Microphone and speaker

Material on "blackboard" can be printed and distributed in hard copy to participants.

23

A petition:
1. Is a formal statement.
2. Is signed by eligible individuals.
3. Asks that a specific action be taken.

25

RESOLUTION

26

REPORT CLASSIFICATIONS

27

TACTICAL PLANS

28

SALES OR PERSUASION
LETTER FORMULA

29

SIMPLIFIED BUSINESS LETTER

30

EMPHASIS TECHNIQUES

26

Reports are classified according to:
1. Type of text or data
2. Time intervals
3. Information flow
4. Context
5. Function
6. Message style

25

Resolutions are:
1. A formal statement expressing appreciation, congratulations or sympathy.
2. Statements from an entire group of people.
3. Written with the word _Whereas_ preceding each reason for the resolution.
4. Written with the word _Resolve_ introducing paragraphs stating action to be taken.

28

The sales/persuasion letter formula is:

A - Attention
I - Interest
D - Desire
A - Action

Sales letters usually are long and use a number of emphasis techniques.

27

Tactical plans outline the actions required of a particular work unit to achieve its part of the total strategic plan.

30

In writing there are a number of ways to emphasize or call attention to information. Some are:
1. Colored paper, ink
2. Font style and point
3. Boxes, indentions
4. Graphics
5. Handwritten messages
6. Underscore
7. Capitalization
8. Bold print, etc.

29

A simplified business letter:
1. Is always in **full block** format.
2. _Never_ has a **salutation.**
3. _Never_ has a **complimentary close.**